The Master Key Budget VOL.3
BLUEPRINT

For more resources, please visit https://www.ofpsagency.com

The Master Key Budget VOL.3
BLUEPRINT

Stacey M. Oliver

Olivers Financial Planning Services, LLC ®™

South Carolina

For more resources, please visit https://www.ofpsagency.com

Disclaimer

The advice contained in this guide may not be suitable for everyone. The author obtained information from sources that may be reliable and from her own experience. The information in this guide is provided for education and informational purposes only, without any express or implied warranty of any kind, including warranties of accuracy, completeness for any particular purpose. The material contained in this guide is not intended to be and does not constitute financial, legal or any other advice. The information is general in nature and is not specific to you the user or anyone else. The author, distributor and publisher particularly disclaims any liability, loss or risk taken by individuals who directly or indirectly act on the information contained herein. All readers must accept all and full responsibilities for their use of this material. All pictures used in this guide are for illustrated purposes only. The pictures are only licensed for use of this guide and must not be used for any other purpose without prior written permission of the rights holder.

Copyrights

Work Cited
(https://en.oxforddictionaries.com/, n.d.)
(https://en.wikipedia.org/wiki/, n.d.)
(https://www.merriam-webster.com/, since 1828)

Printed and Published in the United States of America

The Master Key Budget BLUEPRINT VOL.3
STACEY M. OLIVER

ISBN-13: 978-1-7350929-3-5

Interior Designs by STACEY M. OLIVER

A New Kind of Agency

Olivers Financial Planning Services, LLC

(aka OFPS, LLC) was incorporated and founded by Stacey M. Oliver, CEO, in 2015. Our mission is to create, enlighten, and empower committed effective stewards of finances. Our primary objective is to increase our clients' financial literacy awareness so they can fully understand how money works.

"Money can work hard for you instead of you working hard for it. Once that concept is learned then the vicious cycle and hold of debt can be removed."

Hello

Hi, I'm ***Stacey M. Oliver***, your Financial Locksmith.

I empower individuals with the Master Key to unlocking doors to financial freedom.

Now let me ask...What is keeping the doors locked to you obtaining total financial freedom? The answer is simple, *Barrier(s).* A barrier is an obstacle that prevents movement, access, or progress.

If you do not become empowered with the Master Key to complete financial freedom the trend of financial barriers and financial ignorance will continue to filter and recycle through you and/or your family.

If the financial barrier is not broken and destroyed in our lives, there will not be a financial legacy left for our next generation. Stop allowing the doors to remain locked to your financial freedom. **Possess the Master Key and start taking charge of unlocking doors to your financial wealth so you can begin to experience Financial FREEDOM.**

The Master Key Budget Blueprint workbook will expand your financial knowledge base. A budget plan is an excellent tool to monitor all income (pay) and debts (bills). The decisions you make with your money can be deliberated in advance. This volume is key to your total financial freedom.

The Budget Blueprint (volume 3) will show you the best way to strategize and plan everything, from setting, starting and sticking to a budget. Utilize this manual to assemble your budgetary choices, change your monetary conduct and become a compelling cash administrator.

Table of Contents

BUDGET

"Spending with <u>NO FOCUS</u> equals poverty."

-Stacey M. Oliver

Budget

How many of us maintain a **Budget** to keep track of our obligations and to ensure those obligations are paid timely. A **Budget Plan** is an excellent tool to keep track of all income and expenses. Look at it as an ongoing developing progress.

Be proactive in your planning. The decisions you make with your finances can be deliberated in advance. A lack of budgeting always leads to a lack of money. Remember, budgeting does not limit your income status nor your savings capacity. If you do not save or know where your money is going then you may want to take advantage of a **Budget** plan. Why? A **Budget** will keep you accountable and help you avoid spending outside your means.

Two key factors to budgeting are income and expenses. On the next pages you will find a break down and a variation of income and expenses. Review the terms and take a moment to fill in the appropriate blanks that apply to you.

The final page, **Budget Balance**, allows you to input and subtract the total amount of your expenses and income to determine if your final calculations (balance) are positive or negative number. Hint: You want your end total to always be positive.

Budget Income

Name	
ASSETS	
Income	
Rent Income	
Social Security	
Disability	
Interest Income	
Bonus Income	
Pension	
Dividends	
Other Income	
TOTAL INCOME	$

<u>TERMS</u>

- **Income**: take home pay; payments received for work rendered.
- **Rent Income**: payment received for use of property or land.
- **Social Security**: governmental system providing monetary assistance to individual with an inadequate or no income.
- **Disability**: monthly payments to disabled recipients.
- **Interest Income**: earnings/gains from stock, savings, certificate of deposits, etc.
- **Bonus Income**: extra incentive payments.
- **Pension**: a regular payment made during a person's retirement from an investment fund to which that person or their employer has contributed during their working life.
- **Dividends**: a sum of money paid regularly (typically quarterly) by a company to its shareholders out of its profits (or reserves).

Budget Expenses

Name	Monthly Payment	Qtrly/Annual Payment	Balance	Creditor(Payee)
EXPENSES				
Charitable Donations (Tithe)				
Savings Fund				
Emergency Fund				
College Fund				
Gifts Fund (Birthdays, Anniversaries, Just Because, Holidays, etc.)				
Vacation Fund				
Pay Yourself (Pocket Money)				
Home Mortgage				
2nd Home Mortgage (Equity Line)				
Auto Loan1				
Auto Loan2				
Credit Card 1				
Credit Card2				
Credit Card3				
Credit Card 4				
Loan1 (Installment)				
Loan 2 (Website/Domain)				
Loan3 (Line of Credit)				
Loan4 (Paypal)				
Student Loan				
Alimony / Child Support				
IRS				
Electricity				
Heating Fuel Oil or Natural Gas				
Water & Sewer				
Home Telephone				
Mobile Telephone				
Cable TV (DirecTV, Charter, etc.)				
TOTAL MONTHLY EXPENSES	$	$	$	

Budget Expenses continued...

Name	Monthly Payment	Qtrly/Annual Payment	Balance	Creditor(Payee)
EXPENSES				
Auto Maintenance (Oil Change, Brakes, Tune-Up, Tires, Wash, etc.)				
Auto Insurance				
Auto Tax				
Health Insurance Paid directly (not by employer)				
Life Insurance Paid Directly (not by employer)				
Medical/Dental Expenses (Copays if not w/ER Flex Spending)				
Home Maintenance (Painting, Plumbing, Yard, etc.)				
Homeowner's Insurance (If not included w/Mortgage)				
Renter's Insurance				
Real Estate Tax (If not included w/ Mortgage)				
Land Tax/Lot Payment				
Retirement (If not w/Employer)				
Groceries (Toiletries, Personal Hygiene, etc.)				
Lunch Money(Work, School, etc.)				
School Supplies				
School Trips				
School Dues				
Transportation(Bus/Subway), Parking, Tolls				
Hair Maintenance				
Clothing, Shoes, etc				
Dry Cleaning/Laundry				
Internet Service				
Hobby (Supplies, Vendor Shows, etc.)				
Homeowner's Association Dues				
Recreation/Entertainment Money				
Gas (Automobile, Boat, Motorcycles, etc.)				
Other Expenses				
TOTAL MONTHLY EXPENSES	$	$	$	

Budget Balance

- **If the grand total is positive = NET GAIN**
  Income outweighs Expenses

- **If the grand total is negative = NET LOSS**
  Expenses outweighs Income

Name:	
Total Expenses	$
Total Income	$
GRAND TOTAL (Net Gain/Loss)	$

INCOME – EXPENSES = NET GAIN/LOSS

Test Your Knowledge

To determine if your budget plan balances, the final calculations should be a ________________ number or equals ________________.

Fill in the blanks.

Hint: You want your final calculations (balance) to always be positive.

Positive, Net Gain are the Correct Answers

Getting Back on Track

- **Scenario 1**: During any financial hardships do not avoid your obligations. Contact your creditors to keep them inform of your situation and see if there is a hardship or work out program ideal for your circumstance or situation.

- **Scenario 2**: Bill rotation is helpful when budget plan is off-track. Bill rotation is when bills are rotated every 30 days until payments are brought current. Take two set-bills like auto and installment loan. Both payments are due around the same time but there is not enough money in the budget to pay each bill. Pay one on-time and the other bill before it becomes thirty days past due. *(Note: late fees may apply.)*

- **Scenario 3**: Do not avoid mortgage payments. Contact mortgage servicing company for options like forbearance, loan modification, refinancing, deferment, or repayment plan, etc. Missed mortgage payments have a significantly negative impact on credit score.

- **Scenario 4**: If an unforeseen crisis arises that causes a delay in timely payments consider paying the bills before the next payment is due until bills are back on track. For instance; if auto payment is due on the 5th of every month ensure the bill gets paid before the 5th of the following month so the bill will not be reported as 30 days or more delinquent. *(Note: late fees may apply.)*

Action Plan

Budget Plan from Scratch

Instructions to Start from Scratch

- Starting on page 24, List all **set-bills** first and label as **SB**. set-bills are debts that cannot be changed. In other words, if you do not pay these type of bills the results will be negatively reported and or placed in collections.

- Next list all **unset-bills** and label as **UB**. Unset-bills payment amounts fluctuate based upon usage. *(Unset-bills include water, electric, wireless internet, car taxes, etc.)*

- Then list all **other** expenditures such as entertainment, dining, etc. and label **O**. *(This category can be altered as necessary.)*

- As a result this will allow you to make as many adjustments as needed to create the right budget plan just for you.

Extra worksheets have been added.

Budget Plan from Scratch

BILLS	LABEL (SB/UB/OTHER)	COMMENTS

Budget Plan from Scratch

BILLS	LABEL (SB/UB/OTHER)	COMMENTS

Budget Plan from Scratch

BILLS	LABEL (SB/UB/OTHER)	COMMENTS

Budget Plan from Scratch

BILLS	LABEL (SB/UB/OTHER)	COMMENTS

Budget Plan from Scratch

BILLS	LABEL (SB/UB/OTHER)	COMMENTS

Budget Plan from Scratch

BILLS	LABEL (SB/UB/OTHER)	COMMENTS

Test Your Knowledge

Set-bills change whereas unset-bills do not change an other expenditures are not quiet necessary in most cases.

- ❑ True
- ❑ False

❑ False Correct Answer

Comments

Simple Budget Plan

A sample **Simple Budget Plan** has been provided for you to follow when completing and establishing your budget plan to see if you are spending more than you make.

Extra worksheets have been added for your use as you pay off debt.

Simple Budget Plan

*The easiest way to save is "AUTOSAVE"

MONTHLY BUDGET PLAN						
ASSETS						
Income	$ 2,700.00 (Note: Gross Income $3,100.00)					
EXPENSES						
Obligations	Monthly Amount	BILL AMT TO PAY 1st pay period-15	BILL AMT TO PAY 2nd pay period-30/31	PAYDOWN/PAYOFF	DUE DATE	NOTES
Tithe (10% of Gross Income)	310.00	155.00	155.00			*Due Each Pay Period*
Pay Yourself (3% of Net Income)	81.00	40.50	40.50			*Pay Each Pay Period*
Savings (3% of Net Income)	81.00	40.50	40.50			*Save Each Pay Period*
Mortgage/Rent	1080.00	1080.00			*15th*	
Home Association Dues						
Home Taxes/Insurance						
Duke Power	97.00		97.00		*30th*	
Water	53.00	53.00			*30th*	
Childcare						
Car Ins	77.00		77.00			
Car Payment	404.00		404.00	PAYOFF		
Car Taxes						
Gas	120.00	60.00	60.00			*Fuel Each Pay Period*
Wireless/Internet	76.00		76.00		*30th*	
Cell Phone	111.00		111.00		*30th*	
Family/Children Phone						
Food/Groceries	210.00	105.00	105.00			*Shop Each Pay Period*
Personal Hygiene Products						
Clothing						
Shoes						
Medical/Dental						
Cable						
Hair Barber						
Hair Salon						
Hair/Lashes						
Nail Spa						
Restaurants						
Entertainment						
Vacation						
Other						
Other						
Total Expenses	$ 2,700.00	$ 1,534.00	$ 1,166.00	Note: The red box totals should equal the white box total.		
Total Net Income/Loss (Income minus total Expenses)	$ 0					

SAMPLE

For more resources, please visit https://www.ofpsagency.com

Simple Budget Plan

MONTHLY BUDGET PLAN						
ASSETS						
Income	$					
EXPENSES						
Obligations	Monthly Amount	BILL AMT TO PAY 1st pay period-15	BILL AMT TO PAY 2nd pay period-30/31	PAYDOWN/PAYOFF	DUE DATE	NOTES
Total Expenses	$	$	$	Note: The red box totals should equal the white box total.		
Total Net Income/Loss (Income minus total Expenses)	$					

Simple Budget Plan

MONTHLY BUDGET PLAN

ASSETS

Income	$

EXPENSES

Obligations	Monthly Amount	BILL AMT TO PAY 1st pay period-15	BILL AMT TO PAY 2nd pay period-30/31	PAYDOWN/PAYOFF	DUE DATE	NOTES
Total Expenses	$	$	$	Note: The red box totals should equal the white box total.		
Total Net Income/Loss (Income minus total Expenses)	$					

For more resources, please visit https://www.ofpsagency.com

Simple Budget Plan

MONTHLY BUDGET PLAN

ASSETS

Income	$

EXPENSES

Obligations	Monthly Amount	BILL AMT TO PAY 1st pay period-15	BILL AMT TO PAY 2nd pay period-30/31	PAYDOWN/PAYOFF	DUE DATE	NOTES
Total Expenses	$	$	$	Note: The red box totals should equal the white box total.		
Total Net Income/Loss (Income minus total Expenses)	$					

Simple Budget Plan

MONTHLY BUDGET PLAN

ASSETS

Income	$

EXPENSES

Obligations	Monthly Amount	BILL AMT TO PAY 1st pay period-15	BILL AMT TO PAY 2nd pay period-30/31	PAYDOWN/PAYOFF	DUE DATE	NOTES
Total Expenses	$	$	$	Note: The red box totals should equal the white box total.		
Total Net Income/Loss (Income minus total Expenses)	$					

Simple Budget Plan

MONTHLY BUDGET PLAN						
			ASSETS			
Income	$					
			EXPENSES			
Obligations	Monthly Amount	BILL AMT TO PAY 1st pay period-15	BILL AMT TO PAY 2nd pay period-30/31	PAYDOWN/PAYOFF	DUE DATE	NOTES
Total Expenses	$	$	$	Note: The red box totals should equal the white box total.		
Total Net Income/Loss (Income minus total Expenses)	$					

For more resources, please visit https://www.ofpsagency.com

Simple Budget Plan

MONTHLY BUDGET PLAN

ASSETS

Income	$

EXPENSES

Obligations	Monthly Amount	BILL AMT TO PAY 1st pay period-15	BILL AMT TO PAY 2nd pay period-30/31	PAYDOWN/PAYOFF	DUE DATE	NOTES
Total Expenses	$	$	$	Note: The red box totals should equal the white box total.		
Total Net Income/Loss (Income minus total Expenses)	$					

For more resources, please visit https://www.ofpsagency.com

Simple Budget Plan

MONTHLY BUDGET PLAN						
ASSETS						
Income	$					
EXPENSES						
Obligations	Monthly Amount	BILL AMT TO PAY 1st pay period-15	BILL AMT TO PAY 2nd pay period-30/31	PAYDOWN/PAYOFF	DUE DATE	NOTES
Total Expenses	$	$	$	Note: The red box totals should equal the white box total.		
Total Net Income/Loss (Income minus total Expenses)	$					

For more resources, please visit https://www.ofpsagency.com

Simple Budget Plan

MONTHLY BUDGET PLAN						
ASSETS						
Income	$					
EXPENSES						
Obligations	**Monthly Amount**	**BILL AMT TO PAY 1st pay period-15**	**BILL AMT TO PAY 2nd pay period-30/31**	**PAYDOWN/PAYOFF**	**DUE DATE**	**NOTES**
Total Expenses	$	$	$	Note: The red box totals should equal the white box total.		
Total Net Income/Loss (Income minus total Expenses)	$					

For more resources, please visit https://www.ofpsagency.com

Simple Budget Plan

MONTHLY BUDGET PLAN						
ASSETS						
Income	$					
EXPENSES						
Obligations	Monthly Amount	BILL AMT TO PAY 1st pay period-15	BILL AMT TO PAY 2nd pay period-30/31	PAYDOWN/PAYOFF	DUE DATE	NOTES
Total Expenses	$	$	$	Note: The red box totals should equal the white box total.		
Total Net Income/Loss (Income minus total Expenses)	$					

Simple Budget Plan

MONTHLY BUDGET PLAN						
ASSETS						
Income	$					
EXPENSES						
Obligations	**Monthly Amount**	**BILL AMT TO PAY 1st pay period-15**	**BILL AMT TO PAY 2nd pay period-30/31**	**PAYDOWN/PAYOFF**	**DUE DATE**	**NOTES**
Total Expenses	$	$	$	Note: The red box totals should equal the white box total.		
Total Net Income/Loss (Income minus total Expenses)	$					

Simple Budget Plan

MONTHLY BUDGET PLAN						
ASSETS						
Income	$					
EXPENSES						
Obligations	Monthly Amount	BILL AMT TO PAY 1st pay period-15	BILL AMT TO PAY 2nd pay period-30/31	PAYDOWN/PAYOFF	DUE DATE	NOTES
Total Expenses	$	$	$	Note: The red box totals should equal the white box total.		
Total Net Income/Loss (Income minus total Expenses)	$					

For more resources, please visit https://www.ofpsagency.com

Simple Budget Plan

MONTHLY BUDGET PLAN						
ASSETS						
Income	$					
EXPENSES						
Obligations	Monthly Amount	BILL AMT TO PAY 1st pay period-15	BILL AMT TO PAY 2nd pay period-30/31	PAYDOWN/PAYOFF	DUE DATE	NOTES
Total Expenses	$	$	$	Note: The red box totals should equal the white box total.		
Total Net Income/Loss (Income minus total Expenses)	$					

Budget Plan Recommendations

It is important to keep your expenses at least 60% or less of your income (net pay/take home pay).

The other 40% is to be allocated as following:

10% = Contribution
10% = Pay Yourself
10% = Savings
10% = Emergency Fund

To determine if your expenses fall within or below the 60% perimeter use this simple equation:

Total Expenses ÷ Total Net Pay = %

Action Plan

Quick Reminders

Budget Plan Recommendations

Budget Control

- ✓ Open two separate accounts (checking).
  1) Bill Account
  2) Spending Account
- ✓ Set up auto-draft payments.
- ✓ Do NOT spend bill money for pleasure in hopes of paying it back later.
- ✓ Do NOT count your eggs before they hatch. In other words, Do NOT count your money before it's earned or received.
- ✓ Save extra funds/checks received unintentional or unexpected.
- ✓ Make plans to spend or buy.
- ✓ Avoid including bonuses and any other extra income within the budget for expenses.
- ✓ When planning a budget only consider your main income if possible.

Action Plan

Quick Reminders

Budget Plan Recommendations

Avoid Late Payments

- ✓ Utilize a calendar for on-time bill payments.
- ✓ Call lender to set up payment arrangements if unforeseen circumstance arises.
- ✓ Establish a new routine of paying bills.
- ✓ Call lender and request due date change.
- ✓ Make paying bills on-time top priority.
- ✓ Automate payments.
- ✓ Identify and change bad payment habits.
- ✓ Ask revolving creditors about hardship programs.

Quick Reminders

Action Plan

Savings

Jump Start

- Open savings account at separate bank from your regular checking account (for example; an online savings account).
- Save coins (piggy bank, empty containers/water bottles).
- Price shop comparison.
- Look for ways to save money (couponing, weekly ads, discounts, deals such as BOGO etc.).
- Do NOT grocery shop hungry.
- Make a shopping list.
- Shop off seasons.
- Know when to buy in bulk.

Quick Reminders

401K Investments

Things to Know

- When is 401k fully vested as of the participation starting date?
- Contribute to the MAX of the company's match contribution.
- Does the plan include a safe harbor investment option?
- What qualifies as a hardship withdrawal?
- Does the plan provide loan options?

Action Plan

Quick Reminders

ACCOUNT LOG SHEET

"Unlock the door of your mind with the key of KNOWLEDGE." –Stacey M. Oliver

Account Log

	WEBSITE LINK	ACCOUNT#	*USERNAME*	*PASSWORD*
LOANS				
EXAMPLE: World Finance	https://www.loansbyworld.com/	987456321	JonDoe1	3JoN!Do3
CREDIT CARDS/LINE OF CREDIT				
UTILITIES				
AUTO INSURANCE				

Account Log

	WEBSITE LINK	ACCOUNT#	*USERNAME*	*PASSWORD*
LOANS				
CREDIT CARDS/LINE OF CREDIT				
UTILITIES				
AUTO INSURANCE				

Account Log *continued...*

	WEBSITE LINK	ACCOUNT#	*USERNAME*	*PASSWORD*
PERSONAL BANK ACCOUNTS				
BUSINESS BANK ACCOUNTS				
INVESTMENTS AND RETIREMENT				
LIFE INSURANCE				

Comments

GLOSSARY
&
RESOURCES

Glossary

- **Assets**: valued property or item an individual owns free and clear.
- **Bonus Income**: extra incentive payments.
- **Budget**: map or plan of all monies expected to earn or receive and how it will be saved or spent: a way of goal setting or paying down or paying off debt: the amount of money that is available for, required for, or assigned to a particular purpose.
- **Credit Card**: open-end loans with a certain limit used by individuals to pay for everyday expenses/purchases or provide cash advances to be paid over a period of time which may incur interest on any outstanding loan balance.
- **Disability**: monthly payments to disabled recipients.
- **Dividends**: a sum of money paid regularly (typically quarterly) by a company to its shareholders out of its profits (or reserves).
- **Expenses**: money spent to buy or pay for something; bill payments.
- **Income**: take-home pay: total receipt of money from work or service rendered, investments, etc.

Glossary

- **Installment Loan**: typically for big ticket items such as home, vehicles, etc.
- **Interest Income**: earnings/gains from stock, savings, certificate of deposits, etc.
- **Liabilities**: money owed: outstanding balance for secured or unsecured loans and purchases bought on credit.
- **Minimum payment**: lowest dollar amount required to be paid each month on a loan, credit card, or other debt.
- **Net Gain/Net Income**: the positive balance once the expenses have been subtracted from the income.
- **Net Loss**: the negative balance once the expenses have been subtracted from the income.
- **Online banking**: managing your bank or credit union accounts through a secure website: bill paying method set up with a bank or credit union.
- **Pension**: a regular payment made during a person's retirement from an investment fund to which that person or their employer has contributed during their working life.
- **Rent Income**: payment received for use of property or land.

Glossary

- **Secured Loan**: loans in which property owned by individuals are used as collateral.
- **Social Security**: governmental system providing monetary assistance to individual with an inadequate or no income.
- **Unsecured Loan**: no property is used for collateral (most common type is credit cards).

Resources *continued...*

Annual Credit Report Link:
https://www.annualcreditreport.com/index.action

Credit Cards:
https://www.creditcards.com/rewards-cards/

Equifax Link: www.equifax.com

Experian Link: www.experian.com

FICO Score Link: https://creditscorecard.com/

Identity Theft: https://www.identitytheft.gov/Assistant

Opt-Out Online Link: https://www.donotcall.gov/default.aspx

Reward Cards for Points (Compare Cards by Lending Tree): https://www.comparecards.com/reward?utm

Time Calculator Link:
https://www.timeanddate.com/date/timeduration.html

TransUnion Link: www.transunion.com

Budget Plan Notes

Calendar

MONTH ______________________ YEAR ______________

Sunday	Monday	Tuesday	Wednesday	Thursday	Friday	Saturday

Budget Plan Notes

Calendar

MONTH ______________________________ **YEAR** ________________

Sunday	Monday	Tuesday	Wednesday	Thursday	Friday	Saturday

Budget Plan Notes

Calendar

MONTH ______________________ **YEAR** ____________

Sunday	Monday	Tuesday	Wednesday	Thursday	Friday	Saturday

Budget Plan Notes

Calendar

MONTH ______________________ YEAR ______________

Sunday	Monday	Tuesday	Wednesday	Thursday	Friday	Saturday

Budget Plan Notes

Calendar

MONTH ______________________ **YEAR** ____________

Sunday	Monday	Tuesday	Wednesday	Thursday	Friday	Saturday

Budget Plan Notes

Calendar

MONTH ______________________				YEAR ____________		
Sunday	Monday	Tuesday	Wednesday	Thursday	Friday	Saturday

Budget Plan Notes

Calendar

MONTH ______________________ **YEAR** ______________

Sunday	Monday	Tuesday	Wednesday	Thursday	Friday	Saturday

Budget Plan Notes

Calendar

MONTH ______________________ **YEAR** ______________

Sunday	Monday	Tuesday	Wednesday	Thursday	Friday	Saturday

Budget Plan Notes

Calendar

MONTH ______________________ YEAR ______________

Sunday	Monday	Tuesday	Wednesday	Thursday	Friday	Saturday

Budget Plan Notes

Calendar

MONTH ______________________				YEAR ______________		
Sunday	Monday	Tuesday	Wednesday	Thursday	Friday	Saturday

Budget Plan Notes

Calendar

MONTH ______________________ **YEAR** ______________

Sunday	Monday	Tuesday	Wednesday	Thursday	Friday	Saturday

Budget Plan Notes

Calendar

MONTH ______________________________ **YEAR** ________________

Sunday	Monday	Tuesday	Wednesday	Thursday	Friday	Saturday

Quick Reminders

Take Action

TO DO LIST

Priority	Due Date	What	Who	In Progress	Done

NOTES:

For more resources, please visit https://www.ofpsagency.com

Take Action

TO DO LIST

Priority	Due Date	What	Who	In Progress	Done

NOTES:

Take Action

TO DO LIST

Priority	Due Date	What	Who	In Progress	Done

NOTES:

Stay Connected

Olivers Financial Planning Services, LLC
(aka OFPS, LLC)

www.ofpsagency.com

https://instagram.com/oliversfps

http://www.twitter.com/Ofpsllc

http://www.facebook.com/Oliversfps

Olivers Financial Planning Services, LLC ®TM
PO Box 51363
Piedmont, SC 29673
Email: ofpsagency@outlook.com

Made in United States
North Haven, CT
04 November 2026

21723865R00058